Doodle Tiles

This Doodling book was made with your creativity in mind.

There are two Blank tiles per book leaf.

This is so you don't have to worry abut the ocassional beleed thru as well as being able to cut the tile out to use in scrapbooking projects if you want.